Social Media

Connect with a community of *Bible Studies for Life* users. Post responses to questions, share teaching ideas, and link to great blog content. *Facebook.com/BibleStudiesForLife*

Get instant updates about new articles, giveaways, and more. **@BibleMeetsLife**

The App

Simple and straightforward, this elegantly designed iPhone app gives you all the content of the Small Group Member Book—plus a whole lot more—right at your fingertips. Available in the iTunes App Store; search **"Bible Studies for Life."**

Blog

At *BibleStudiesForLife.com/blog* you will find all the magazine articles we mention in this study guide and music downloads provided by LifeWay Worship. Plus, leaders and group members alike will benefit from the blog posts written for people in every life stage—singles, parents, boomers, and senior adults—as well as media clips, connections between our study topics, current events, and much more.

Connected: My Life in the Church
Bible Studies for Life: Small Group Member Book

© 2014 LifeWay Press

ISBN: 978-1-4300-3426-1

Item: 005672342

Dewey Decimal Classification Number: 254.5

Subject Heading: CHURCH MEMBERSHIP \ CHURCH RENEWAL \ CHURCH GROWTH

Eric Geiger
Vice President, Church Resources

Ronnie Floyd
General Editor

David Francis
Managing Editor

Gena Rogers
Sam O'Neal
Content Editors

Philip Nation
Director, Adult Ministry Publishing

Faith Whatley
Director, Adult Ministry

Send questions/comments to: Content Editor, *Bible Studies for Life: Adults*, One LifeWay Plaza, Nashville, TN 37234-0175; or make comments on the Web at *www.BibleStudiesforLife.com*

Printed in the United States of America

For ordering or inquiries, visit www.lifeway.com; write LifeWay Small Groups; One LifeWay Plaza; Nashville, TN 37234-0152; or call toll free (800) 458-2772.

All Scripture quotations, unless otherwise indicated, are taken from the Holman Christian Standard Bible®, copyright 1999, 2000, 2002, 2003, 2009 by Holman Bible Publishers. Used by permission.

Bible Studies for Life: Adults often lists websites that may be helpful to our readers. Our staff verifies each site's usefulness and appropriateness prior to publication. However, website content changes quickly so we encourage you to approach all websites with caution. Make sure sites are still appropriate before sharing them with students, friends, and family.

I am a Christian. Therefore, I am connected.

Let's make a quick list of pressing issues we face on a regular basis:

▶ Paying the bills

▶ Raising a family

▶ Keeping afloat in today's economy

▶ Church membership

Church membership? I doubt the issue of church membership makes it on most people's list, but it should. Unfortunately, many Christians have developed a faulty view of what it means to be a church member. Many of us talk about our church in terms of what we get out of it. This consumer mentality focuses on the perks we gain from the church, which makes church membership sound more like club membership.

In reality, being part of the body of Christ means so much more.

The Book of Ephesians helps us see the true benefits that come from our connections to Christ and His church. Within this study we'll discover six ways that church members are connected: connected in Christ, connected in unity, connected in growth, connected through words, connected in service, and connected through prayer.

Your connection to the church—your membership—will prove over time to be just as important as paying the bills and raising a family. During this study you'll discover that, through Christ, we are all truly connected in a way that lasts not just for a lifetime, but for all eternity.

Thom S. Rainer

Dr. Thom S. Rainer serves as president and CEO of LifeWay. One of his greatest joys is his family: his wife Nellie Jo; his three sons, Sam, Art, and Jess; and his seven grandchildren.

Dr. Rainer publishes a daily blog at *ThomRainer.com* and can be followed on Twitter *@ThomRainer*. He has authored several books, including the book that complements this study: *I Am a Church Member: Discovering the Attitude that Makes the Difference.*

contents

SESSION 1

CONNECTED IN CHRIST

When have you been interested to join a group or a cause?

QUESTION #1

#BSFLChrist

Church membership is a privilege made possible through Christ.

THE BIBLE MEETS LIFE

Membership has its privileges.

Join Yellowstone Club in Big Sky, Montana, and you can golf, ski, snowboard, ride horseback, fly fish, hike, bike, kayak, and more among some of the most beautiful scenery in the country. You can dine in luxury. You may even rub elbows with celebrities. Of course, you'd expect these kinds of perks from a club that requires $300,000 to join and $30,000 in annual dues—and that's after you buy a multi-million dollar condo, mansion, or ranch.

Most people can't relate to forking over millions of dollars for such perks, but we do get the idea of membership. We've all belonged to organizations where we pay our dues and are entitled to certain benefits in return. The problem occurs when we bring this same mentality to the church. Church membership isn't about having our needs met, but there is great value in being a church member.

Let's begin our study with an important truth from the Book of Ephesians—that belonging to the body of Christ is a gift.

WHAT DOES THE BIBLE SAY?

Ephesians 2:17-22 (HCSB)

17 When the Messiah came, He proclaimed the good news of peace to you who were far away and peace to those who were near.

18 For through Him we both have access by one Spirit to the Father.

19 So then you are no longer foreigners and strangers, but fellow citizens with the saints, and members of God's household,

20 built on the foundation of the apostles and prophets, with Christ Jesus Himself as the cornerstone.

21 The whole building, being put together by Him, grows into a holy sanctuary in the Lord.

22 You also are being built together for God's dwelling in the Spirit.

Key Words

Foreigners, strangers (v. 19)—"Foreigners" refers to non-citizens who are short-term in a country; "strangers" to longer term residents. Neither had citizenship or full rights.

Cornerstone (v. 20)—The foundation stone that anchors the whole structure. It sets the angle and the bearings for the structure that will rise from the foundation.

Ephesians 2:17-18

If you or I went to the White House in Washington D.C. and requested an audience with the president, we'd likely receive a formal reply that could be translated as, "Yeah, right." It wouldn't happen. Not for ordinary citizens like us. But if the president's wife or children appeared with the same request, the response would be different. Of course they have unqualified access to the president—they're his family!

To put things in perspective, Ephesians 2:17-18 is not about the elected leader of any one country. It's about the sovereign, eternal Ruler of the universe. We may not have access to the U.S. president, but we do have access to God.

In Ephesians 2, Paul wrote that at one time the believers had been far away from God (see 2:13). He reminded them they had been disobedient, living in sin, and subject to God's anger (see vv. 1-3). They were without hope and without God in the world (v. 12). Cut off. No access. Excluded.

But then Jesus arrived. When He died on the cross to pay the penalty for sin, He made a way for those who were separated from God to be reconciled to Him. Jesus opened the door and gave the excluded— which includes us—access to God. The gift of salvation is for all who believe in Jesus and trust Him as their Savior.

What emotions do you experience when you think about having direct access to God?

QUESTION #2

Scripture makes it clear: no one can earn this right standing with God by his or her own good deeds. "For you are saved by grace through faith, and this is not from yourselves; it is God's gift—not from works, so that no one can boast" (Eph. 2:8-9).

By grace alone, we who had no relationship with God have now become sons and daughters with unlimited access to the Ruler of the universe. We're family. We're in!

The Lord of the universe is on His throne conducting business, while you and I are given access to enter and sit at His feet. We were undeserving, rebellious sinners who now have the greatest access imaginable. And that access is a gift.

How is being part of a church like being part of a family?

QUESTION **#3**

YOUR IDEAL MEMBERSHIP

Create a membership card that would improve your life right now.

Use the questions provided to help set the parameters of that membership.

1. What will you gain?

2. Who can use it?

3. How much will it cost?

4. How long will it last?

Ephesians 2:19

Beginning a relationship with God is a little like going through one of those turnstiles to enter a football stadium—it happens one person at a time. God saves us as individuals. We each must come to Him through personal faith. But once we enter that relationship with Him, we immediately become part of His family.

Before coming to Christ, the Ephesians were outsiders. By dying on the cross, however, Jesus made a way for them to become a part of His family. Now, through their faith, they were joined with all believers—Jew and Gentile. Instantly, they went from being outsiders to being insiders. Access to God gave them access to the family of God.

I remember my own entry into God's family when I was a teenager. My high school football coach, Joe Hendrickson, showed me the Bible verse, "For all have sinned and fall short of the glory of God" (Rom. 3:23). He explained that everyone is a sinner, and none of us deserves salvation. We all deserve death (see Rom. 6:23). Coach Hendrickson helped me understand that Jesus took the punishment for me with His death on the cross (see 2 Cor. 5:21).

After hearing my coach explain the gospel, I repented of my sins and placed my faith in Jesus (see Acts 3:19). At that moment, I received the gift of salvation, which included forgiveness of my sins and adoption by God the Father. It meant the Holy Spirit came to dwell in me. And it made me part of the body of Christ. Just as it was for the first century Gentile Ephesian believers, so it is for all of us: membership in the body of Christ, the church, is a gift from God.

As a gift, membership in the body of Christ is something to be treasured. It's not a legalistic obligation. It's not a country club to provide us privileges and perks. It's not a license for entitlements. It is a gift to be cherished.

> *What prevents us from viewing church membership as a privilege?*
>
> QUESTION #4

Ephesians 2:20-22

Country clubs, health clubs, and the like exist primarily for one purpose: they are businesses designed to make a profit for the owner. So if you choose to join a club, it makes sense to consider what it will cost, what activities and services it will provide, and how well you like the other members.

By contrast, the church is not a business. It is the body of Christ, with Jesus as the head. The church is built on the foundation of the apostles who witnessed the life, death, and resurrection of Jesus and declared His gospel. The church is not primarily for us; the church is for God, who founded it and sustains it to this day.

Paul called Jesus Christ the chief cornerstone of the church. In ancient architecture, the chief cornerstone was the most important stone in a building, more important even than the foundation. Covering a right angle where two walls joined, it was the binding stone that held the entire structure together. To say Jesus is the church's chief cornerstone is to say that everything in and about the church rests on His authority. In other words, Jesus is the reason for the church's existence. He is the One who connects us all together. The purpose of the church is to worship and serve Him.

God never intended His church to be a place for followers to act like consumers seeking to be served and entertained. Instead, He designed the church to be a missionary people carrying out the greatest work the world has ever known. Therefore, an invitation to join with Jesus and His followers in carrying out that mission is truly a gift that should inspire our humble gratitude and motivate our sacrificial service.

Jesus remains the foundation of the church. What is our role in continuing His work?

QUESTION #5

LIVE IT OUT

Ephesians 2 helps us understand what the church is. So how do you apply this truth in your life?

▶ **View church membership as a gift.** Thank God daily for the opportunity to be included in His family, the church.

▶ **Ask the right question.** John F. Kennedy famously challenged Americans, "Ask not what your country can do for you, ask what you can do for your country." This week, ask your pastor, "What can I do for my church?"

▶ **Invite others in.** Identify those around you who need to be introduced to the gospel and included in Christ's church. Invite at least one of these individuals to church this week.

Church membership isn't about our needs. It's about meeting the needs of others. Most importantly, it's about serving the one true God. Yes, membership certainly has its privileges.

He'll Come Running

There's a dangerous temptation many of us face when we think we've got God all figured out. I've noticed that I tend to get myself into all kinds of trouble when I make assumptions about how He moves and leave no room for mystery. We walk a fine line when we assume that God must think and feel and respond as we do. God is "other," unlike us in so many ways.

To continue reading "He'll Come Running" from *HomeLife* magazine, visit *BibleStudiesforLife.com/articles.*

My group's prayer requests

_____

_____

_____

_____

_____

_____

_____

_____

_____

_____

My thoughts

SESSION 2

CONNECTED IN UNITY

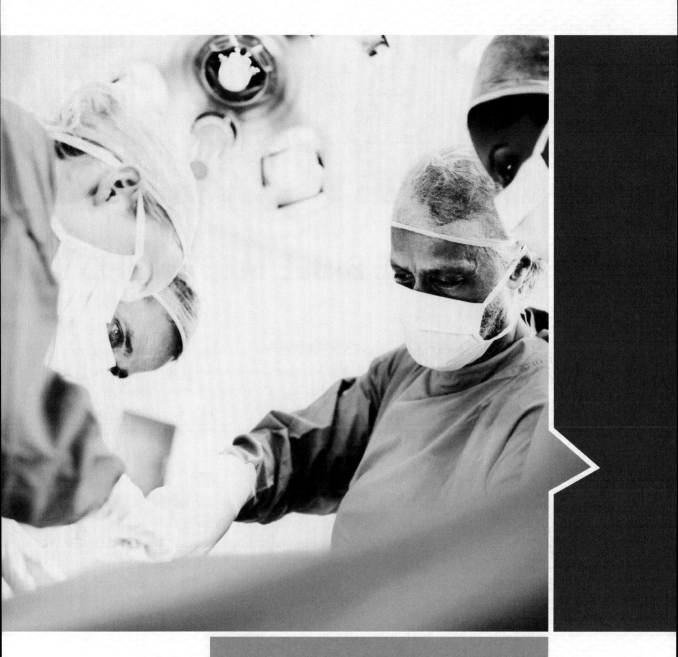

When have you been in a situation where working together was a necessity, not an option?

QUESTION #1

#BSFLunity

> *Unity is a given, but staying unified takes work.*

THE BIBLE MEETS LIFE

"Let's roll."

Those two words became the rallying cry of our nation in one of its darkest hours. On the same morning terrorists crashed commercial airplanes into the World Trade Center towers and the Pentagon, they also hijacked United Flight 93 with the goal of destroying another target. When passengers and crew members realized what was happening, they pulled together as a group and stormed the cabin to thwart the terrorists' plot.

"Let's roll" was the phrase that signaled the beginning of that final, courageous act. Travelers from different backgrounds, races, and age groups set aside their differences and bonded together for a common mission. United by their urgent goal, they selflessly disregarded personal safety to work as one. They became heroes.

What if the church operated with such courage and resolve? No, we don't always agree. But we can still set aside our differences, sacrifice our personal comfort, and work together to fulfill our call.

WHAT DOES THE BIBLE SAY?

Ephesians 4:1-6 *(HCSB)*

1 Therefore I, the prisoner for the Lord, urge you to walk worthy of the calling you have received,

2 with all humility and gentleness, with patience, accepting one another in love,

3 diligently keeping the unity of the Spirit with the peace that binds us.

4 There is one body and one Spirit—just as you were called to one hope, at your calling—

5 one Lord, one faith, one baptism,

6 one God and Father of all, who is above all and through all and in all.

Key Words

Humility and gentleness (v. 2)—"Humility" is the lowliness of spirit that enables one to defer to others. "Gentleness" is the meekness that enables restraint rather than overbearing use of strength.

Ephesians 4:1-2

God clearly wants His children to get along. His will is for Christians to be unified. But unity doesn't just happen within a group of people simply because they all decided to join the same church. Unity takes work. It takes sacrifice. It requires individuals who recognize they can serve as a unifying or divisive force within the body—and choose to seek unity.

Paul emphasized this choice in Ephesians 4:1-2 when he challenged his readers about the way they treated one another. He pleaded with them to live in a manner worthy of their calling as members of God's kingdom. The word translated "worthy" in the original language typically referred to balance, as in the balancing of scales. In essence, Paul was saying, "Let your actions equal what you profess."

The same principle applies to those of us in the church today. If we say we are following Jesus, our treatment of other believers ought to corroborate our testimony, not conflict with it.

So, how should we treat one another today as followers of Christ? Paul laid out several characteristics in verse 2: humility, gentleness, patience, and loving acceptance.

Gentleness is linked with humility. Being gentle isn't the same as being a doormat. It isn't being weak or cowardly. Rather, it involves showing kindness. It means being considerate of others. Those who are gentle don't demand their own way or grasp for power. Jesus showed gentleness by welcoming little children who wanted to be near Him (see Matt. 19:14). He was gentle when He offered encouragement rather than condemnation to the woman caught in adultery (see John 8:10-11).

In addition to humility and gentleness, Paul called for patience among believers. Patience carries the idea of putting up with others' faults and failures and not seeking revenge when wronged—which goes hand in hand with accepting one another in love. It's the willingness to forgive and not bear a grudge. It's the Christlike view that says: "I see your imperfections, but I love you anyway. I forgive you because God has forgiven me."

Each of these attributes is vital to maintaining unity within the church.

> **What in these verses do you find most difficult to apply?**

QUESTION **#2**

HAVE PATIENCE?

What helps you demonstrate patience in these and other frustrating situations?

Ephesians 4:3

Paul never said maintaining unity in the church would be easy. In fact, he anticipated it would be difficult. That's why he emphasized the importance of hard work in verse 3. Paul's words convey the necessity of striving with determination to overcome obstacles for the sake of unity.

We need the power of God's Spirit living within us to enable us to consistently respond to others with gentleness and humility. The Spirit helps us to bear patiently with others' faults and forgive when we are wronged. In other words, the Spirit makes us one, and the Spirit empowers us to maintain unity by guiding us to think and act like Jesus. Therefore, by staying attuned to the Spirit, we remain in tune with one another. When we're controlled by the Spirit, we avoid actions and attitudes that creep into the church and destroy unity.

Unforgiveness is an enemy of church unity. Holding onto hurt feelings until they grow into bitterness is like nursing cancerous cells in the body of Christ. Refusing to let go of anger is a sure way to create divisions and sow discord. For these reasons, Paul urged the Ephesians to deal with their anger promptly before it could produce destruction (see Eph. 4:26).

Forgiveness isn't easy. It may require us to let go of resentment over and over—every time anger rears its ugly head. But those who truly comprehend the depth of their own sins and the wonder of God's grace can never withhold forgiveness from others.

The common denominator of any action that interrupts unity in the church is selfishness. The desire to get the upper hand on others runs counter to the work of the Holy Spirit. But it takes work to put aside our own interests and serve others. Unity requires that we are diligent about living in the peace given to the church through the presence of the Spirit.

> *Why does staying unified require so much effort?*
>
> QUESTION **#3**

> *Since churches are diverse, what unifies us as the body of Christ?*
>
> QUESTION **#4**

Ephesians 4:4-6

Why is unity so important? Because we have a mission to complete as the body of Christ (see Matt. 28:18-20), and we can't complete that mission as individuals. We need one another. Unity is critical.

But beyond the need for teamwork, there's a very real sense in which believers are spiritually bound together. We've been designed to live the Christian life in connection with the body of Christ. In fact, Paul used the word "one" seven times to explain the different elements that tie us to one another as the church.

▶ Though made up of individual Christians, the church exists as **one body**.

▶ Within the church you will find people of all ages, races, classes, and more. We are completely diverse, but **one Spirit** indwells us all.

▶ The Spirit's dwelling within us is our guarantee of the **one hope** we share (see 2 Cor. 1:22). Our common hope is that we who trust in Jesus Christ will spend eternity with Him in heaven.

▶ Christians are bound together by **one Lord, one faith, one baptism**. We're united by our common belief that Jesus alone is Savior (see John 14:6). We proclaim this belief publicly through the symbol of baptism.

▶ All Christians worship the **one God**, who is the Creator and Sustainer of the universe. The "oneness" of God is the foundation for our unity as the church.

> *What steps can we take to model unity in our church and community?*

QUESTION #5

LIVE IT OUT

You have a choice. Your actions this week will contribute to unity or division in the church. With that in mind, here are some practical ways you can apply what you've learned:

▶ **Don't participate in gossip.** Stop gossip when it's shared with you and look for ways to encourage people instead.

▶ **Forgive.** We've all been wronged. Identify any grudges you've been harboring and forgive the people involved.

▶ **Seek forgiveness.** Work with the Holy Spirit to identify ways in which you have contributed to division within your church. Confess your actions and seek forgiveness.

Like the passengers of United Flight 93, we as Christians find ourselves bound together by a purpose larger than ourselves. We have an urgent mission and a divine calling. We have a chance to heroically strive for unity in the body of Christ.

Walk the Line

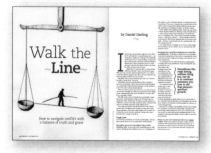

I was having a particularly rough day at the office, and I carelessly left a weapon lying around—my email inbox. Chafed at a colleague who publicly embarrassed me in a team meeting, I composed a bitter and sarcastic email and, without hesitation, clicked "Send." Then I propped up my feet on the desk and waited for the smoke cloud to rise from the office of my perceived enemy.

To continue reading "Walk the Line" from *HomeLife* magazine, visit *BibleStudiesforLife.com/articles*.

My group's prayer requests

....

....

....

....

....

....

....

....

....

....

My thoughts

SESSION 3

CONNECTED
IN GROWTH

What do you like best about being a fan?

QUESTION *#1*

#BSFLgrowth

Church members need one another in order to grow in Christ.

THE BIBLE MEETS LIFE

"Roll Tide!"

I am a fan of the University of Alabama Crimson Tide. Notice I did not say I am a *member* of the Crimson Tide—there's a difference. I don't go to spring practices and work out with the team. I don't study game films or discuss plays with the coaches. On game day, I don't get on the field and help the team move the ball across the goal line. That's not my job. I'm a fan—a spectator. I buy my ticket and cheer for my team from the stands or watch them play on television.

Thankfully, church membership is not like football. There should be no spectators. The body of Christ wasn't designed to operate as an organization where the supporters come and give their money and then watch the hired players do all the work. We're all participants. Everyone has a role to play. Everyone is needed. That's how the body of Christ grows and fulfills its mission.

As we'll see in this session, the question is not: "*Do* I have a role in the church?" The real question is: "*What's* my role in the church?"

WHAT DOES THE BIBLE SAY?

Ephesians 4:11-16 *(HCSB)*

11 And He personally gave some to be apostles, some prophets, some evangelists, some pastors and teachers,

12 for the training of the saints in the work of ministry, to build up the body of Christ,

13 until we all reach unity in the faith and in the knowledge of God's Son, growing into a mature man with a stature measured by Christ's fullness.

14 Then we will no longer be little children, tossed by the waves and blown around by every wind of teaching, by human cunning with cleverness in the techniques of deceit.

15 But speaking the truth in love, let us grow in every way into Him who is the head—Christ.

16 From Him the whole body, fitted and knit together by every supporting ligament, promotes the growth of the body for building up itself in love by the proper working of each individual part.

Key Words

Fitted and knit together (v. 16)—"Fitted" translates a compound word based in part on the root for harmony. Together the phrase reflects a properly working and smoothly functioning whole.

Ephesians 4:11-12

Jesus supplies the church with people He has gifted in various ways to fill all the roles needed for the church's mission. The roles mentioned in Ephesians 4:11 do not make up an exhaustive list of leadership positions within the church, but they are important.

▶ **Apostles and prophets.** These leaders made up the foundation of the early church. The apostles had been with Jesus during His ministry or had witnessed His post-resurrection appearances. The prophets preached the gospel.

▶ **Evangelists.** People in the church tasked with sharing the gospel and seeking a response to it.

▶ **Pastors and teachers.** These roles likely were combined or complementary; they involved nurturing, protecting, feeding, and supervising the flock.

Church leaders are not gifted to do all the work of the ministry themselves. They are gifted so that they can train the saints—that's all the rest of us as believers—to do the work of ministry. Every member has a function in the body of Christ. Either you're doing the work of the ministry or you're equipping others to do the work of the ministry in some form or fashion. Those are the only options.

The word translated "training" in verse 12 carries the idea of restoring something to its original condition or making something complete. This kind of training, equipping, or perfecting is needed to prepare believers for service in doing God's work.

Paul understood his role as an equipper of other believers. He wrote to the Colossians, "We proclaim Him, warning and teaching everyone with all wisdom, so that we may present everyone mature in Christ" (Col. 1:28). Paul delegated tasks, enlisted people to pray for him, and relied on the help of coworkers.

In other words, Paul understood his role as a servant of Christ. He understood that every member has a role to play in the body of Christ.

> *When have you felt fully equipped to carry out an important task?*

QUESTION **#2**

> *What obstacles keep us from equipping others or being equipped ourselves?*

QUESTION **#3**

Ephesians 4:13

Remember when you were a kid and couldn't wait to grow up? Maybe you longed for the day you'd turn 13 and officially become a teenager. Or you dreamed of your 16th birthday and that prized driver's license. But then you realized 18 was the age when society would finally recognize you as an adult. And then you yearned to be 22, finished with college, and on your way to the "real world."

We should also strive for spiritual maturity as believers in the body of Christ. God provides His children with various gifts so we can help one another grow. In Ephesians 4:13, Paul said God's goal in providing His church with workers—apostles, prophets, evangelists, pastors, and teachers—is to build up the church so that we all reach unity in the faith and knowledge of Jesus and become mature.

How do we assess our spiritual growth? How do we measure maturity? The answer comes in verse 13: "With a stature measured by Christ's fullness."

The life of Christ is our target. It was Paul's consuming goal to know Christ more, to know the power of His resurrection, and to share in the fellowship of His suffering (see Phil. 3:10). He wrote, "Not that I have already reached the goal or am already fully mature, but I make every effort to take hold of it because I also have been taken hold of by Christ Jesus" (Phil. 3:12).

Therefore, we measure our spiritual maturity by gauging our actions and attitudes in comparison with the actions and attitudes of Christ. Jesus lived to please God. He put others above Himself. He patiently endured suffering. He loved the unlovable and forgave the undeserving. That's our goal for spiritual growth and maturity. Thankfully, we don't work toward that goal on our own. God equips His people with gifts that enable them to help one another grow to be like His Son.

> **What does it look like to measure spiritual maturity based on the fullness of Christ?**
>
> QUESTION #4

Ephesians 4:14-16

Having a poor foundation in the truth of Scripture makes you susceptible to all kinds of false teachings that can lead you away from God. This is another reason we need one another within the church. Paul constantly battled false teachers who infiltrated churches and led people astray. His remedy, identified in Ephesians 3:11-14, was to ensure churches were built up with mature believers grounded in the truth. Knowing the truth is key to discerning falsehood. In Ephesians 4:15, he contrasted the lies and deceit of false teachers with the importance of believers speaking the truth in love.

Speaking the truth in love means being honest with people about realities such as sin and how God views our rebellion against Him. It means we communicate that message with humility, but it also means we don't compromise the teachings of Scripture when it comes to essentials of our faith—essentials such as:

▶ Jesus is the only way to salvation.

▶ We can't save ourselves by our own good works.

▶ We can only be made righteous by repenting of our sin and trusting in Jesus for our forgiveness.

▶ God expects His children to live holy lives.

With Christ as the head of the church and with each member working together in submission to Him, the whole body gets stronger.

> *What advice would you give someone seeking to balance speaking truth and showing love?*

QUESTION #5

"The concept of an inactive church member is an oxymoron."

—THOM RAINER, *I AM A CHURCH MEMBER*

WHO HELPED **YOU GROW?**

Record the names of individuals who contributed to your spiritual growth during the following seasons of life.

Childhood:

....

Adolescence:

....

Adulthood:

....

How are you currently contributing to the spiritual growth of others?

LIVE IT OUT

You have a responsibility to equip others for ministry or engage in ministry yourself. Here are some practical ways to fulfill that responsibility and join the movement toward spiritual growth:

▶ **Be a participator, not a spectator.** Identify a specific and practical way to serve others in your church and community.

▶ **Get equipped.** With the Holy Spirit as your guide, seek out someone older and wiser you can ask to pour into your life as a spiritual mentor.

▶ **Balance your speech.** When issues or conflicts arise during the week, make a conscious effort to speak the truth in a way that also demonstrates love.

What's your role in the church? Answering that question is key to getting on the field and helping your team—the body of Christ—strive for growth and spiritual victory in the world today.

Daddy Warhide

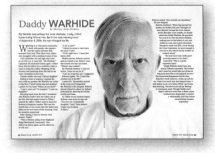

Zig Warhide was perhaps the most obstinate, cranky, critical human being I'd ever met. But in the early morning hours of September 8, 2000, this man changed my life. Working in a retirement community, I dealt with people who appreciated the many activities that enriched their lives. Then there were others who struggled with a profound sense of loss. I still remember the call light that went on at 2:30 a.m. in room 257. "Mr. Warhide," I groaned.

To continue reading "Daddy Warhide" from *Mature Living* magazine, visit *BibleStudiesforLife.com/articles.*

My group's prayer requests

....

....

....

....

....

....

....

....

....

....

My thoughts

SESSION 4

CONNECTED THROUGH WORDS

**What is your favorite way
to share good news?**

QUESTION #1

#BSFLwords

> *Our words matter.*

THE BIBLE MEETS LIFE

"Sticks and stones will break my bones, but words will never hurt me."

It's not true. You and I both know words can be harmful. You and I can both remember a time—maybe even a time recently—when someone said something that slipped past our defenses and struck home. Maybe it was a casual comment. Maybe it was a direct attack. Either way, we can still feel the emotional wound where those words cut with the sharpness of a knife.

Yes, words can hurt us. Words can wreak havoc. But words can also be a powerful force for good. Words can motivate, encourage, and inspire. They can bring hope into darkness and change the direction of a life. This is especially true in the church.

As we'll see in this session, our words have great impact on how we relate to one another as followers of Christ.

WHAT DOES THE BIBLE SAY?

Ephesians 4:25-32 *(HCSB)*

25 Since you put away lying, Speak the truth, each one to his neighbor, because we are members of one another.

26 Be angry and do not sin. Don't let the sun go down on your anger,

27 and don't give the Devil an opportunity.

28 The thief must no longer steal. Instead, he must do honest work with his own hands, so that he has something to share with anyone in need.

29 No foul language is to come from your mouth, but only what is good for building up someone in need, so that it gives grace to those who hear.

30 And don't grieve God's Holy Spirit. You were sealed by Him for the day of redemption.

31 All bitterness, anger and wrath, shouting and slander must be removed from you, along with all malice.

32 And be kind and compassionate to one another, forgiving one another, just as God also forgave you in Christ.

Key Words

Redemption (v. 30)—The Greek term means "liberation by ransom." Jesus paid the ransom price on the cross to secure our spiritual redemption from sin for those who trust Him.

> **What is your initial reaction to Paul's commands about honesty and anger?**

QUESTION #2

Ephesians 4:25-28

The church is a body of individuals bound together in a common mission to advance God's kingdom. For that reason, those inside the church should live in a way that's noticeably different from those outside.

For example, Paul encouraged his readers to be truthful. I recently heard about a survey in which 547 business professionals were asked, "Is it ever OK to lie at work?" Most of the respondents said it's OK to lie in some situations. Specifically, they said it's OK to lie when being honest would be perceived as a "career limiting" move. They also felt lying was justified when people in management were less than honest, or when lies were necessary to cover up errors in business cultures that don't allow for mistakes.[1]

As a society, we've also become adept at practicing deception even as we "technically" tell the truth—we simply omit certain details or fail to mention key facts. We justify deception by categorizing it as a "white lie" or a "necessary evil."

Such actions are devastating in the church. Dishonesty destroys trust and unity within the body of Christ.

Paul also warned his readers about anger. Notice he didn't say we should avoid anger altogether. Instead, he gave these instructions for when we get angry:

▶ Don't sin.

▶ Don't let the sun go down on your anger.

▶ Don't give the Devil an opportunity.

There are different ways to handle anger when it comes. For example, many people stew in their anger, replaying the offenses that provoked them, looking for ways to justify their rage. The problem is that feeding anger this way provides the Devil an opportunity to tempt us toward bitterness, hatred, and revenge. That's why this passage says to settle disagreements before sunset.

The better choice is to go to the person who angered you and seek peace as quickly as possible. Choose to forgive. Words hurt, remember? And words spoken in anger can be especially damaging in the church.

How does a church benefit when its members speak with integrity?

QUESTION #3

BE ANGRY. DON'T SIN?

Circle any of these words that cause you to feel angry.

HUNGER DRUGS CRIME
POLITICS WALL STREET CONGRESS
DIVORCE BANKRUPTCY POLICE
GLOBAL WARMING DECEPTION
GOSSIP FACEBOOK HYPOCRISY

How can the commands in verses 25-32 influence the ways you deal with anger?

Ephesians 4:29-30

Ever try putting toothpaste back inside the tube after you've squeezed it out? It's virtually impossible. Words work the same way. Once spoken, they can't be taken back. Yes, you can apologize, but you can't un-say something that's been said. Harsh words can leave an emotional mark on others just like a physical blow leaves a bruise.

Paul warned the Ephesian believers to choose their words carefully when communicating with one another. In verse 29, he warned them specifically against using foul language with one another. The word translated "foul" refers to something rotten, such as spoiled food.

We tend to think of foul language in terms of cursing or saying something inappropriate. Certainly that kind of speech dishonors God and undermines our Christian witness. But in the context of these verses, Paul's reference to unwholesome talk has more to do with malicious gossip and slander. He was referring to speech that inflicts harm on someone and causes division within the body—speech that tears down spiritually and emotionally rather than building up.

Rather than tearing others down, let's be intentional about using words to build one another up—especially within the body of Christ. Think back to when someone spoke the right words to you at the right time. We value such encouragement. As representatives of God's kingdom, we must be intentional about speaking words that encourage others and help them grow. In this way, we serve as channels of God's grace, allowing Him to minister through us and provide what our brothers and sisters in Christ need to hear.

Paul also warned against grieving the Holy Spirit—a caution all Christians should take seriously. We have the opportunity to please God when we use words that build one another up within His church. At the same time, we possess the ability to disappoint God and grieve His Spirit when we use words to tear one another down.

> *How does technology amplify the impact of our words?*

QUESTION #4

Ephesians 4:31-32

A family is driving to church when a discussion about the checkbook quickly becomes a full-blown argument. By the time they arrive at the church, everyone is frustrated and upset. When they get out of the car, however, everyone looks polished and happy. They smile and pretend like nothing is wrong.

What are we to make of such behavior? The answer is that we often compartmentalize our lives. One compartment holds "church life," while other compartments reveal how we *really* operate.

The Christian life doesn't work that way. It makes no sense to profess our love for Jesus in one setting and then verbally abuse or gossip about others in another. James wrote, "Praising and cursing come out of the same mouth. My brothers, these things should not be this way" (Jas. 3:10). To follow Jesus Christ requires that we relate to others the way He relates to us. Because God showed us kindness and compassion—because He forgave us when we didn't deserve it—we must treat others the same way.

In Ephesians 4:31, Paul told his readers to get rid of ungodly attitudes and actions such as bitterness, anger, wrath, shouting (clamor), slander (evil speaking), and malice. Paul concluded the chapter with an admonition to show kindness and compassion, and to forgive one another the way God forgives us.

One word characterizes this kind of speech: loving. As followers of Jesus and members of His church, everything we say and do should be based on the foundation of love.

LIVE IT OUT

Choosing to speak in a positive way seems easy, but it can be difficult to accomplish. Here are some options for being wise with your words:

▶ **Speak positively.** Look for opportunities where your words can encourage, motivate, give hope, provide guidance, or even just make someone smile.

▶ **Memorize Psalm 19:14.** Pray this verse every morning as you prepare for the day ahead. Let it guide your speech.

▶ **Resolve your dishonesty.** Identify a person with whom you've been dishonest in recent months. Confess your deception, request forgiveness, and affirm your commitment to honest speech moving forward.

Words can certainly hurt us. That's the truth. But words can also be a powerful force for good. That's our hope. Choose to bring hope into darkness and connect others with Christ through your words.

All to Jesus, I Surrender

I found my healing in the church. After a few months of running the other way, I finally shared the shame of my past abortion with a woman in my new church. She immediately took me to Scripture that equally revealed God's redeeming love. Little did I know that God would someday use the most shameful part of my past to unfold His plans for my future.

To continue reading "All to Jesus, I Surrender" from *Mature Living* magazine, visit *BibleStudiesforLife.com/articles.*

My group's prayer requests

....

....

....

....

....

....

....

....

....

....

My thoughts

[1] Carol Kinsey Goman, *"When It's OK to Tell Lies at Work,"* forbes.com, 04 Feb. 2013.

SESSION 5

CONNECTED IN SERVICE

What is something you always wanted but never got?

QUESTION *#1*

Serving in the church is not about what I want.

THE BIBLE MEETS LIFE

It's not about us.

Have you ever wondered what it takes to meet the demands of a diva? For one rock star, those demands include a 200-person entourage with 30 bodyguards, personal chefs, a yoga instructor, an acupuncturist, and an on-site dry cleaner. This person needs 20 international phone lines and lots of flowers in the dressing room—lilies and roses (white and light pink only) with stems trimmed to exactly 6 inches. Oh, and the hotel room must be emptied of all furniture, because she ships her own furniture directly from home.

"Outrageous!" we say. Yet Christians sometimes approach church life with a similar mentality. We expect the church to cater to our preferences and serve our needs. Sometimes we even get angry and threaten to leave when things don't go our way.

Today we'll explore what the church might be like if members focused less on getting what we want and concentrated more on serving others.

WHAT DOES THE BIBLE SAY?

Ephesians 5:15-21 *(HCSB)*

15 Pay careful attention, then, to how you walk—not as unwise people but as wise—

16 making the most of the time, because the days are evil.

17 So don't be foolish, but understand what the Lord's will is.

18 And don't get drunk with wine, which leads to reckless actions, but be filled by the Spirit:

19 speaking to one another in psalms, hymns, and spiritual songs, singing and making music from your heart to the Lord,

20 giving thanks always for everything to God the Father in the name of our Lord Jesus Christ,

21 submitting to one another in the fear of Christ.

Key Words

Filled by the Spirit
(v. 18)—"Spirit" here is the Holy Spirit, the third person of the Trinity. Being filled with the Spirit reflects being under His leadership and empowerment.

Ephesians 5:15-17

Paul urged church members to avoid foolishness and live wisely. Of course, everyone *wants* to be wise. We don't intend to act foolishly. But you may be surprised at the level of foolishness present in today's churches. My research team conducted a survey in which they questioned churches identified as self-serving and inwardly focused.[1] The results revealed 10 behavior patterns of members in such churches:

1. **Worship wars:** Church members clash over music styles, instrumentation, and order of service.

2. **Prolonged minutia meetings:** Leaders spend an inordinate amount of time in meetings.

3. **Facilities focus:** The church places a high priority on protecting rooms and furniture.

4. **Program driven:** Programs become an end instead of a means to greater ministry.

5. **Inwardly focused budget:** A disproportionate share of the budget is used for the needs and comforts of church members rather than reaching people outside the church.

6. **Inordinate demands for pastoral care:** Church members place unreasonable expectations on the pastor and staff to care for them—even when they have no significant need.

7. **Attitudes of entitlement:** Church members act as if they deserve special treatment.

8. **Greater concern about change than the gospel:** Church members get fired up if you move their classroom, but they don't care much about participating in the work of the gospel.

9. **Anger and hostility:** Members regularly express hostility toward staff and other members.

> *Who has been a model of wisdom in your life?*

QUESTION #2

10. Evangelistic apathy: Members care more about their own needs than the greater eternal needs of the world and community around them.

These patterns are foolish because they work against our mission as church members and followers of Christ. We need to live wisely, which means serving others in a way that's motivated by God's priorities, not our personal wants and comfort.

> *What are the implications of being filled by the Spirit on a daily basis?*

QUESTION #3

SPENDING TIME

Create a pie chart to show how you spend your time during a typical day.

What are some ways to incorporate serving others into each section of your day?

....

....

....

....

....

....

Ephesians 5:18

It's our nature to be selfish. It's our nature to want others to serve us rather than be the servants. So how do we make the change to live wisely among our brothers and sisters in the body of Christ? Is it just a matter of stiffening our resolve and willing ourselves to serve whether we like it or not?

No. According to Paul, the answer lies not in seeking greater control, but in *surrendering* control to the Holy Spirit (v. 18). Daily submission to the Spirit helps us bear the fruit of the Spirit—love, joy, peace, patience, kindness, goodness, faith, gentleness, and self-control (see Gal. 5:22-23)—in our relationships.

To "be filled" with the Spirit is to be controlled and empowered by Him—but it's not a one-time event. The verb suggests continuous action. It really means to "go on being filled," indicating a daily process of submission to the Spirit. Just as Jesus said His followers must deny themselves, take up their cross daily, and follow Him (see Luke 9:23), we must daily surrender control of our lives to the Spirit. The Spirit then motivates us to make God's priorities our passions.

Look at the example of the early Christians. The Spirit showed His presence and power in their lives when church members sold their possessions and shared daily with those in need (see Acts 2:44-45; 4:32-37). The first Christians were characterized by an attitude of willing self-sacrifice in which generosity won out over selfishness. The early Christians were also serious about sharing their faith (see Acts 2:14-41). God's priorities became their priorities, and they were driven by a passion to share the gospel.

Likewise, when we live under the influence of the Spirit, we will serve others, give generously, and share our faith rather than focus on getting what we want out of church. We'll be empowered to live as God wants us to live when we submit to His Spirit.

> *"We will never find joy in church membership when we are constantly seeking things our way."*
>
> —THOM RAINER, *I AM A CHURCH MEMBER*

What changes must we make in order to serve the way God wants?

QUESTION **#4**

Ephesians 5:19-21

In verses 19-21, Paul described the influence of the Holy Spirit in our lives. Believers filled by the Spirit choose to fill their speech with praises for God (v. 19), continually give thanks to God (v. 20), and submit to one another (v. 21). These three attributes are the opposite of entitlement.

Being filled by the Holy Spirit affects the way we live each day—it changes our actions and attitudes. We experience a genuine appreciation for what God has done in us and through us, we recognize that we're undeserving recipients of God's grace and mercy, and we live in a state of continual wonder at everything we've been given. Such an attitude of praise and gratitude compels us not only to serve God, but also to serve one another.

Jesus, the Servant King, set the ultimate example for how to humble ourselves this way. The cross was not Jesus' preference (see Luke 22:42), but He declined His preferences, desires, and comfort—and He did it for our benefit. To follow Jesus is to do the same for our brothers and sisters in His body, the church.

All Christians are to practice submission. Now, it's easy for us to say "I'll submit when she submits" or "I'll sacrifice after he sacrifices." But we're not responsible for the way others behave—even other Christians in the church. We're responsible for the way we behave. Therefore, we don't have to wait for others in the church to submit, serve, or offer genuine praises to God. We can take the first steps in obedience to Christ and through the influence of His Spirit.

What does it mean to submit to one another in the context of a local church?

QUESTION **#5**

LIVE IT OUT

Are you a giver or a taker in the body of Christ? Here are some practical ideas for engaging your church the right way:

▶ **Assess yourself.** Look again at the patterns of self-centered churches (listed on pp. 48-49). Take a moment to consider whether you contribute to any of these patterns in your church.

▶ **Accentuate the positive.** Make a list of everything you like best about your local church.

▶ **Jump in.** Work with leaders at your church to identify a ministry in which your service will meet a need. Then take the plunge and serve with wisdom.

Submission is countercultural in the world today, which means it can be tough to bend our will to God's Spirit—and especially to other members in the body of Christ. But it's worth it. Because the church is not about us.

Put on a Yes Face

A friend once told me he could classify every person he met into one of two categories—those with a "yes" face and those with a "no" face. Intrigued with his assertion, I immediately set out to put it to the test. For the next month, every time I walked through a mall or an airport, I would look at each person who walked by and ask myself: Does this person have a yes face or a no face? The results were informative.

To continue reading "Put on a Yes Face" from *Mature Living* magazine, visit *BibleStudiesforLife.com/articles*.

My group's prayer requests

....

....

....

....

....

....

....

....

....

....

My thoughts

[1] Thom Rainer, *I Am a Church Member* (B&H Publishing Group, 2013), pp. 36-38.

SESSION 6

CONNECTED THROUGH PRAYER

What do you miss most when the power goes out?

QUESTION #1

#BSFLprayer

Support your church with prayer.

THE BIBLE MEETS LIFE

"I'll pray for you."

Author Philip Yancey tells about a Chinese pastor who regularly leads converts in public baptism on the banks of a river, even after spending 20 years in prison because of his faith in Christ. Everyone present at these events understands their participation in baptism could lead to arrest and imprisonment. Yancey asked the pastor, "What can Christians in the rest of the world do for you?" The pastor replied: "You can pray. Please tell the church to pray for us."[1]

Hearing this, Yancey wanted to respond: "Yes, of course, but we honestly do want to help. What else can we do?" In time, he learned that Christians who have no access to earthly power believe prayer gives them access to a greater power. They understand we are engaged in a battle against spiritual forces (see Eph. 6:12).

In this session, we will look at the importance of praying for one another in the church. Biblical church membership calls for Christians to regularly intercede for their brothers and sisters in Christ.

WHAT DOES THE BIBLE SAY?

Ephesians 6:18-22 (HCSB)

18 Pray at all times in the Spirit with every prayer and request, and stay alert in this with all perseverance and intercession for all the saints.

19 Pray also for me, that the message may be given to me when I open my mouth to make known with boldness the mystery of the gospel.

20 For this I am an ambassador in chains. Pray that I might be bold enough in Him to speak as I should.

21 Tychicus, our dearly loved brother and faithful servant in the Lord, will tell you all the news about me so that you may be informed.

22 I am sending him to you for this very reason, to let you know how we are and to encourage your hearts.

Key Words

Mystery of the gospel
(v. 19)—The gospel, the good news of new life through faith in Jesus, was once hidden, a mystery. God has now made it known, though it remains a mystery to many.

Ephesians 6:18

If our purpose as a church were simply to socialize, we could thrive on our own steam. But the church is the body of Christ on assignment to accomplish the greatest mission the world has ever known. Plus, we have a vicious enemy trying to defeat us at every turn (see 1 Pet. 5:8). For these reasons and more, we need prayer.

In Ephesians 6:10-17, Paul advised believers to put on the full armor of God as preparation to engage in spiritual warfare. After describing the equipment necessary to fight such a battle, Paul gave this word on how to win: pray. Specifically, he called for his readers to:

▶ **Pray at all times.** Maintain a continuous dialog with God (see 1 Thess. 5:16). We should be aware that God is always accessible to us, and we should continually reach out to Him.

▶ **Pray in the Spirit.** We are to communicate with God through the Holy Spirit's power. As we do so, the scope and variety of our communication should be wide enough to encompass every kind of need as we pray all kinds of prayers and present to God every request.

▶ **Pray with all perseverance.** This means we don't intercede for others once or twice and then forget about it. We're encouraged to keep asking, keep seeking, and keep knocking (see Luke 11:9-10) because God honors our persistence.

The type of prayer Paul had in mind was intercession: praying for other believers. When we love our brothers and sisters in Christ, we actively want the best for them. We intercede for them through prayer because we believe there are no limits on what God can provide.

How does the command to pray at all times influence our daily routines?

QUESTION #2

Ephesians 6:19-20

When Paul wrote this letter, he was a prisoner awaiting trial in Rome. Yet his request wasn't that he be released or spared. Instead, he asked the Ephesians to pray that he would speak the right words with boldness and share the gospel even in chains. Paul knew he would have a hearing before the Roman authorities, perhaps even in the presence of the emperor. Because his ministry calling was to take the gospel "before the Gentiles and their kings" (Acts 9:15), Paul viewed this audience with Rome's rulers as an ideal opportunity to fulfill God's mission for him.

I find it interesting that even Paul needed God's help to say the right words at the right time and to speak boldly. Paul believed God would act in response to the prayers of fellow Christians interceding on his behalf. Paul craved the prayers of his fellow church members.

Spiritual leaders are prime targets for Satan's attacks. If he can bring leaders down, he can negatively impact others in the kingdom of God. Here are some practical suggestions for interceding on behalf of your pastors and other church leaders:

▶ **Pray for their preaching and teaching.** Pray that God will give them wisdom, insight, and words to speak.

▶ **Pray for their families.** Pastors often struggle with neglecting their families due to church demands. They agonize over criticism of their family.

▶ **Pray for protection.** Ask God to strengthen church leaders against temptation toward greed, adultery, anger, and other sins the Devil would use to destroy their ministry.

▶ **Pray for physical and mental health.** Ask God to fill church leaders with wisdom and discernment so they can lead well and make sound decisions.

> *What keeps us from being more aware of our church leaders' prayer needs?*

QUESTION **#3**

Ephesians 6:21-22

Paul's request for prayer was a common theme in his letters to the early churches (see Rom. 15:30; Col. 4:3-4; and 2 Thess. 3:1-2). And if Paul needed prayer to participate in the mission of the church, surely you and I can benefit by praying for the members of our churches—and by asking them to pray for us.

Maybe you're wondering: *How can I know what to pray for when I'm interceding for others?* The answer is that you must make an effort to stay abreast of how you can pray for your fellow church members. In fact, that's one of your responsibilities as a church member.

Of course, it's ideal when brothers and sisters in Christ take the initiative to request prayer for specific needs. It's also helpful when churches have systems in place to quickly and appropriately make the congregation aware of situations requiring prayer. It was for this reason that Paul sent Tychicus to the Ephesians and other churches—to encourage them, and to let them know how they could pray for Paul's needs.

The speed and accessibility of modern communication means our ability to stay informed of prayer needs is truly limitless. Here are a few ways you can stay connected and pray for others:

> ▶ Touch base with the people you're praying for to find out what's going on in their lives. Visit, call, email, or write. Invest time to move past the surface and find out their spiritual needs and goals.

> ▶ Write down prayer requests so you can pray persistently and go back later to ask for updates.

> ▶ Access resources from mission organizations to learn how missionaries are spreading the gospel throughout the U.S. and across the world—and about the different ways you can pray for them.

> *How do we discern who or what to pray about?*
>
> QUESTION #4

> *How can we use the tools at our disposal to more fully support each other through prayer?*
>
> QUESTION #5

"Because my pastor cannot do all things in his own power, I will pray for his strength and wisdom daily."

—THOM RAINER, *I AM A CHURCH MEMBER*

TIME TO **PRAY**

Look back at the pie chart you created on page 49. Recreate the chart to represent how you will spend your time during a typical day this week.

How will you incorporate prayer into each section of your day?

....

....

....

....

....

....

LIVE IT OUT

God works through the prayers of His people. Therefore, consider these practical ways to pray for your brothers and sisters in Christ:

▶ **Pray for salvation.** Many people miss the benefits of church membership because they are not part of the church. Pray for the salvation of at least one person who needs it.

▶ **Pray for church leaders.** Commit to pray five minutes each day for your pastor(s) and church leaders. (*Note: this works best when you ask them for prayer requests.*)

▶ **Become educated about at least one missionary's needs.** Pray for that missionary and his or her work every day for at least one month.

Prayer grants us access to the power and presence of God. When we believe that, "I'll pray for you" becomes a solemn responsibility and a life-changing promise within the body of Christ.

Heart of the Matter

Through their son's unexpected health crisis, Matt Hammitt, lead singer of the award-winning band Sanctus Real, and his wife, Sarah, rediscovered the meaning of childlike faith.

"I don't know if you've ever experienced a time in your life when a single moment changes everything and takes you down a new path: 'Something is wrong with your baby's heart.' In that moment, my life changed. After I heard those words, a flood of thoughts and questions rushed through my head, and they haven't stopped yet."

To continue reading "Heart of the Matter" from *HomeLife* magazine, visit *BibleStudiesforLife.com/articles*.

My group's prayer requests

....

....

....

....

....

....

....

....

....

....

My thoughts

[1] Philip Yancey, *Prayer: Does It Make Any Difference* (Zondervan, 2006), p. 117.

Connected: My Life in the Church

What a great joy it is to come to Christ and have a personal relationship with Him. As we've seen through this study, our relationship with Christ also brings us into a relationship with other believers. We are connected to one another. We are the bride of Christ and the body of Christ.

Christ

There is no church without Jesus Christ. He is both the head of the church and its only foundation. Because of the work of Christ, we have a relationship with Him and with all others who have a relationship with Him.

Community

By its very definition, community refers to a group of people who share something in common. The church is a community that shares a common faith in Christ. No believer can fully function, grow, or serve Christ apart from the community of faith.

Culture

When people from different backgrounds and ethnicities come together in a community of faith, it gets the world's attention. Despite our differences, we are one in Christ, and the world has no basis for understanding that. Our unity as a church points to Christ.

LEADER GUIDE

CONNECTED

GENERAL INSTRUCTIONS

In order to make the most of this study and to ensure a richer group experience, it's recommended that all group participants read through the teaching and discussion content in full before each group meeting. As a leader, it is also a good idea for you to be familiar with this content and prepared to summarize it for your group members as you move through the material each week.

Each session of the Bible study is made up of three sections:

1. THE BIBLE MEETS LIFE.

An introduction to the theme of the session and its connection to everyday life, along with a brief overview of the primary Scripture text. This section also includes an icebreaker question or activity.

2. WHAT DOES THE BIBLE SAY?

This comprises the bulk of each session and includes the primary Scripture text along with explanations for key words and ideas within that text. This section also includes most of the content designed to produce and maintain discussion within the group.

3. LIVE IT OUT.

The final section focuses on application, using bulleted summary statements to answer the question, *So what?* As the leader, be prepared to challenge the group to apply what they learned during the discussion by transforming it into action throughout the week.

For group leaders, the *Connected* Leader Guide contains several features and tools designed to help you lead participants through the material provided.

QUESTION 1—ICEBREAKER

These opening questions and/or activities are designed to help participants transition into the study and begin engaging the primary themes to be discussed. Be sure everyone has a chance to speak, but maintain a low-pressure environment.

DISCUSSION QUESTIONS

Each "What Does the Bible Say?" section features at least four questions designed to spark discussion and interaction within your group. These questions encourage critical thinking, so be sure to allow a period of silence for participants to process the question and form an answer.

The *Connected* Leader Guide also contains follow-up questions and optional activities that may be helpful to your group, if time permits.

DVD CONTENT

Each video features Eric Geiger interviewing Dr. Thom Rainer about the primary themes found in the session. We recommend that you show this video in one of three places: (1) At the beginning of group time, (2) After the icebreaker, or (3) After a quick review and/or summary of "What Does the Bible Say?" A video summary is included as well. You may choose to use this summary as background preparation to help you guide the group.

The Leader Guide contains additional questions to help unpack the video and transition into the discussion. For a digital Leader Guide with commentary, see the "Leader Tools" folder on the DVD-ROM in your Leader Kit.

SESSION ONE: CONNECTED IN CHRIST

The Point: Church membership is a privilege made possible through Christ.

The Passage: Ephesians 2:17-22

The Setting: Paul penned the Letter to the Ephesians from prison, probably in Rome. He had invested a great deal of time in Ephesus, having visited there briefly near the end of his second missionary journey and spending three years in the city on his third journey. In Ephesus, Christianity confronted both other religions and Greek philosophies. Paul wrote to clarify "church"—what it is, how one enters it, and how one behaves as part of it.

QUESTION 1: When have you been interested to join a group or a cause?

> *Optional activity:* Instruct participants to look through their purses and wallets for membership cards. These can be library cards, club memberships, grocery store discount programs—anything that grants a person access to a specific place or service. Have group members display their cards as they feel comfortable, and then conclude the activity by asking for volunteers to share which membership cards they have found most useful, and why.

Video Summary: This first video message focuses on the background of Ephesians 2. Paul wrote this passage as a reminder that not only have we been made one with Christ, but we have been made one with one another. At the time these words were penned, the concept of oneness was new to the Jews and Gentiles who had never viewed themselves as connected with each other. This concept is also foreign in our day in many ways. We are a disconnected society, but as believers we are united with Christ as well as with others. This is both a privilege and responsibility provided to us through Christ.

WATCH THE DVD SEGMENT FOR SESSION 1, THEN USE THE FOLLOWING QUESTIONS AND DISCUSSION POINTS TO TRANSITION INTO THE STUDY.

- Are there times when connecting with others in Christ feels foreign or awkward to you? Explain.

- Truly connecting with others in the body of believers points us back to what it is to be like Christ. How have you seen this to be true in your life, either through serving others or through being served?

WHAT DOES THE BIBLE SAY?

ASK FOR A VOLUNTEER TO READ ALOUD EPHESIANS 2:17-22.

Response: What's your initial reaction to these verses?

- What do you like about the text?

- What questions do you have about these verses?

TURN THE GROUP'S ATTENTION TO EPHESIANS 2:17-18.

QUESTION 2: What emotions do you experience when you think about having direct access to God?

The idea behind this question is to move group members to consider the power and awe behind this access. It is immediate and direct but only possible through Jesus. Before group members can identify any associated emotions they must understand the reality of the passage. That is, Jesus has made access to God possible for all of us—both near to and far from Him.

> *Optional follow-up:* How have your emotional reactions to God's presence changed over time?

MOVE TO EPHESIANS 2:19.

QUESTION 3: How is being part of a church like being part of a family?

This is an interpretation question included to help group members examine the aspects of being part of "God's household" and its implications. This encourages discussion around a concept familiar to most people—family—that also has application to church membership.

> ***Optional follow-up:*** What are some of the primary differences between being part of a church and being part of a family?

CONTINUE WITH EPHESIANS 2:20-22.

QUESTION 4: What prevents us from viewing church membership as a privilege?

This application question asks group members to examine their own motivations for membership and what stands between them and understanding church membership as a privilege. We are called to serve the body, minister to others, and encourage one another, yet many of us see this as anything but a privilege. This question will help your group become more aware of the conclusions that prevent them from being connected in Christ.

> ***Optional follow-up:*** How have you recently been blessed, uplifted, and encouraged as a member of your church?

> ***Optional activity:*** Direct group members to the activity labeled "Your Ideal Membership" on page 9. Ask for volunteers to describe their ideal membership card.

QUESTION 5: Jesus remains the foundation of the church. What is our role in continuing His work?

The purpose of this question is to help group members identify their roles in continuing His work. Be sure to point out Jesus as the cornerstone and what this means to each of us as members of a church body that is alive and active—not stagnant.

> ***Optional follow-up:*** What obstacles have hindered you from participating more fully in the work of the church?

Note: The following question does not appear in the group member book. Use it in your group discussion as time allows.

QUESTION 6: Dr. Rainer says, "Many churches are weak because we have members who have turned the meaning of membership upside down" (*I Am a Church Member, p.6*). What actions can we take as a group to help define or redefine church membership as a gift and a privilege within our own congregation?

This is an application question for the group to answer as a whole, rather than as individuals. Encourage participation from each member in not only listing ways to define or redefine church membership but acting on it. This is not only asking *how* to live it out, but also *why* your group might change.

LIVE IT OUT

Ephesians 2 helps us understand what the church is. Encourage group members to consider these three options for how to apply this truth:

- **View church membership as a gift.** Thank God daily for the opportunity to be included in His family, the church.

- **Ask the right question.** John F. Kennedy famously challenged Americans, "Ask not what your country can do for you, ask what you can do for your country." This week, ask your pastor, "What can I do for my church?"

- **Invite others in.** Identify those around you who need to be introduced to the gospel and included in Christ's church. Invite at least one of these individuals to church this week.

Challenge: Church membership isn't about our needs. It's about meeting the needs of others. And it's about serving the one true God. But church membership does have privileges. Spend some time this week thinking about what those privileges are. Consider writing them down somewhere as a reminder. Allow those privileges to be a part of what drives you as you serve Christ through your church.

Pray: Ask for prayer requests and ask group members to pray for the different requests as intercessors. As the leader, close this time by committing the members of your group to the Lord and asking Him to help each of you remember that church membership is a privilege and to help you treat it as such.

SESSION TWO: CONNECTED IN UNITY

The Point: Unity is a given, but staying unified takes work.

The Passage: Ephesians 4:1-6

The Setting: Many of Paul's New Testament letters include two broad sections: a theological section where Paul deals with his subject from a doctrinal perspective, followed by a behavioral or ethical section elaborating on how the theology addressed impacts the believer's practice of lifestyle. The ethical/practical section of Ephesians begins at 4:1 and addresses the application of redemption. Paul began the section with an emphasis on the unity the Holy Spirit brings to the church.

QUESTION 1: When have you been in a situation where working together was a necessity, not an option?

Optional activity: Lead participants in a team-building exercise designed to help them experience teamwork. Find two images (at least 8.5 x 11 inches) that are distinct from each other. Cut each image into 10 pieces, and then mix the pieces together in a container. (Note: if you have more than 20 group members, cut the pictures into more pieces.)

Instruct participants to select pieces by passing the container around the group. Each person should have multiple pieces of the pictures. When the container is empty, challenge participants to re-assemble both pictures in less than 5 minutes.

Video Summary: This week's message examines Ephesians 4:1-6, most specifically the use of the word "one" in verses 4-6: "There is **one** body and **one** Spirit—just as you were called to **one** hope at your calling— **one** Lord, **one** faith, **one** baptism, **one** God and Father of all, who is above all and through all and in all." The repetition Paul uses here serves as a reminder that we are one in Christ. Paul understood the importance of unity to the health of the church at that time. And the message he delivered centuries ago remains true in the church today.

WATCH THE DVD SEGMENT FOR SESSION 2, THEN USE THE FOLLOWING QUESTIONS AND DISCUSSION POINTS TO TRANSITION INTO THE STUDY.

- Why do you think unity is important in the church today? Give specific examples.

- How are we unified yet unique?

WHAT DOES THE BIBLE SAY?

ASK FOR A VOLUNTEER TO READ ALOUD EPHESIANS 4:1-6.

Response: What's your initial reaction to these verses?

- What questions do you have about these verses?
- What do you hope to gain from studying about unity in the church?

TURN THE GROUP'S ATTENTION TO EPHESIANS 4:1-2.

QUESTION 2: What in these verses do you find most difficult to apply?

The importance of unity in the church has always been stressed. This self-revelation question is designed to ask group members to identify personal barriers to church unity and explore the reasons behind those barriers.

Optional follow-up: How would you describe the "calling" we have received as followers of Jesus and members of the church?

Optional activity: Direct group members to the activity labeled "Have Patience?" on page 19. Encourage participants to compare their methods for demonstrating patience in difficult circumstances.

MOVE TO EPHESIANS 4:3.

QUESTION 3: Why does staying unified require so much effort?

It's important to allow notions of sin, our worldly nature, and how our culture tends to cater to these aspects of our humanity in this discussion. The "effort" referenced is in place because we must overcome these obstacles.

Optional follow-up: Based on your experience, why is unity worth the effort?

CONTINUE WITH EPHESIANS 4:4-6.

QUESTION 4: Since churches are diverse, what unifies us as the body of Christ?

This interpretation question asks group members to unpack the use of "one" in this passage. You may want to remind them that any time you see the same word so frequently within a passage it requires attention.

Optional follow-up: What actions threaten to interrupt unity?

QUESTION 5: What steps can we take to model unity in our church and community?

Challenge the group to be specific in answering this application question.

Optional follow-up: What is one specific step we will take this week to work for unity within our church and community?

Note: The following question does not appear in the group member book. Use it in your group discussion as time allows.

QUESTION 6: What has our church recently accomplished by working together?

Be prepared to offer some examples of answers to this question.

LIVE IT OUT

You have a choice. Your actions this week will contribute to unity or division in the church. Invite group members to consider these practical ways they can apply what they've learned:

- **Don't participate in gossip**. Stop gossip when it's shared with you and look for ways to encourage people instead.

- **Forgive.** We've all been wronged. Identify any grudges you've been harboring and forgive the people involved.

- **Seek forgiveness.** Work with the Holy Spirit to identify ways in which you have contributed to division within your church. Confess your actions and seek forgiveness.

Challenge: Sometimes conflict and disharmony hit when we least expect it. It's important for us to be prepared when those conflicts come. Spend some time this week devising a game plan for what actions you can take when you see unity being threatened in your area of influence.

Pray: Ask for prayer requests and ask group members to pray for the different requests as intercessors. As the leader, close this time by committing the members of your group to the Lord and asking Him to help each of you contribute to a spirit of unity in your church.

SESSION THREE: CONNECTED IN GROWTH

The Point: Church members need one another in order to grow in Christ.

The Passage: Ephesians 4:11-16

The Setting: Accompanying the unity from the Holy Spirit (session 2) comes the gifting of Christians by Jesus Christ. The gifts given to believers are not, however, for the personal gratification or comparative boasting of the recipients. Instead, He desires that His gifts go toward the mutual growth of the church with the aim that each person reach maturity as measured by Christ's fullness.

QUESTION 1: What do you like best about being a fan?

> *Optional activity:* Bring a collection of DVDs in their cases (or request that group members each come with one of their favorite films). Display the movies so they are visible to participants and then ask for volunteers to answer the question: If you had a chance to star in one role from these movies, which would you choose? *(Note: Be sure to select movies that will not be offensive or distasteful to other group members.)*

Video Summary: Many people think pastors are responsible for doing all the work of ministry in the church when, in fact, Ephesians 4:11-16 shows us that their responsibility is to equip us to join in the work of ministry in and through our churches. As a church we come together for a purpose—to learn the truth, to get to know Him, and to become more like Him. As a result of this equipping, we can go out and do the work we are called to do. A fully-functioning body of Christ is one where everyone is involved in ministry.

WATCH THE DVD SEGMENT FOR SESSION 3, THEN USE THE FOLLOWING QUESTIONS AND DISCUSSION POINTS TO TRANSITION INTO THE STUDY.

- What are the dangers of being involved in the "busyness" of the church versus the business we are called to as a part of the church?

- Why is being grounded in the truth critical for our connectedness to Christ and others?

WHAT DOES THE BIBLE SAY?

ASK FOR A VOLUNTEER TO READ ALOUD EPHESIANS 4:11-16.

Response: What's your initial reaction to these verses?

- What questions do you have about these verses?
- What new application do you hope to get from this passage?

TURN THE GROUP'S ATTENTION TO EPHESIANS 4:11-12.

QUESTION 2: When have you felt fully equipped to carry out an important task?

This question is included to prompt discussion about modeling, training, and teaching. Answers should describe instances during which each group member felt suitably equipped and what made the equipping effective.

> **Optional follow-up:** What emotions do you experience when you don't feel equipped to carry out important tasks? Why?

QUESTION 3: What obstacles keep us from equipping others or being equipped ourselves?

This question is included to fight the notion that church membership is "easy" and doesn't require something from us. As the leader you will want to stress that individual spiritual growth both in ourselves and in other members is a responsibility that belongs to each of us.

> **Optional activity:** Direct group members to the activity labeled "Who Helped You Grow?" on page 31. Ask for volunteers to share about individuals who were especially meaningful in their spiritual development.

MOVE TO EPHESIANS 4:13.

QUESTION 4: What does it look like to measure spiritual maturity based on the fullness of Christ?

Ask the group to look closely at Ephesians 4:13 to consider what the author of Ephesians is revealing about maturity and unity as they engage this question. Specifically examine "unity in the faith," "knowledge of God's Son," "growing into a mature man," and "measured by Christ's fullness."

> **Optional follow-up:** What are some other indicators we often use to assess our spiritual maturity as members of the church?

CONTINUE WITH EPHESIANS 4:14-16.

QUESTION 5: What advice would you give someone seeking to balance speaking truth and showing love?

When answering this application question, keep in mind that speaking truth—even when it is difficult—is crucial to being connected in unity. You might consider asking the group to discuss the many and varied applications of what "speaking truth" in love can mean.

> **Optional follow-up:** When did someone speak the truth to you in love? How did you respond?

Note: The following question does not appear in the group member book. Use it in your group discussion as time allows.

QUESTION 6: How would you describe your role or function within the body of Christ?

You might want to revisit Ephesians 4:11-12 as a part of this discussion. Pay particular attention to ways each group member can be an equipper in addition to being a growing disciple. Be sensitive to visitors, new believers, and non-believers who might not have any frame of reference for responding.

> *Optional follow-up:* How do your God-given gifts and talents support that role or function?

LIVE IT OUT

We have a responsibility to equip others for ministry or engage in ministry ourselves. Encourage group members to consider these practical ways to fulfill their role in their church and join the movement toward spiritual growth:

- **Be a participator, not a spectator.** Identify a specific and practical way to serve others in your church and community.

- **Get equipped.** With the Holy Spirit as your guide, seek out someone older and wiser you can ask to pour into your life as a spiritual mentor.

- **Balance your speech.** When issues or conflicts arise during the week, make a conscious effort to speak the truth in a way that also demonstrates love.

Challenge: What's your role in the church? Answering that question is key to getting on the field and helping your team—the body of Christ—strive for growth and spiritual victory in the world today. Spend some time this week in prayer, asking the Lord to give you a clear vision of His role for you in your church. Consider journaling thoughts and questions you have as well as anything you sense Him telling you through this time.

Pray: Ask for prayer requests and ask group members to pray for the different requests as intercessors. As the leader, close this time by asking the Lord to show each of you your roles and responsibilities in your church.

SESSION FOUR: CONNECTED THROUGH WORDS

The Point: Our words matter.

The Passage: Ephesians 4:25-32

The Setting: As Paul developed the ethical ramifications of the theology of redemption—of being the church—he began with corporate implications (sessions 2 and 3). While all Christians have responsibility for group unity and group maturity, they also have responsibilities for themselves. In this passage Paul pointed out a series of choices each believer should adopt to better facilitate the group unity and maturity.

QUESTION 1: What is your favorite way to share good news?

> *Optional activity:* Help group members pay close attention to their speech by emphasizing the words *good* and *bad* throughout the discussion. Instruct participants to clap once whenever someone says the word *good* at any point. Whenever someone says the word *bad*, participants should clap twice.

Video Summary: This week's video message begins by examining an important aspect of how believers are connected or disconnected through words—the aspect of anger and how we choose to handle it. Righteous anger can be defined as anger toward the things that anger God. Righteous anger holds no grudges, harbors no bitterness. Unrighteous anger camps out in selfishness and personal preferences. Unrighteous anger disconnects and divides churches. Our words are powerful. And it is with our words we either destroy or we build up.

WATCH THE DVD SEGMENT FOR SESSION 4, THEN USE THE FOLLOWING QUESTIONS AND DISCUSSION POINTS TO TRANSITION INTO THE STUDY.

- In what ways does a right understanding of the gospel motivate you to treat others well?

- It was mentioned in the video message that "Christ is our pattern" for how to treat others as well as "Christ is our power." What do those things mean to you?

WHAT DOES THE BIBLE SAY?

ASK FOR A VOLUNTEER TO READ ALOUD EPHESIANS 4:25-32.

Response: What's your initial reaction to these verses?

- What do you like about the text?

- What new application do you hope to receive about the power of your words?

TURN THE GROUP'S ATTENTION TO EPHESIANS 4:25-28.

QUESTION 2: What is your initial reaction to Paul's commands about honesty and anger?

This question asks group members to look deeper into the passage and respond to this call to watch our words, emotions, and reactions. Prompt the group for specific instances or examples in their answers.

Optional follow-up: Do you find it easy or difficult to "Be angry and do not sin"? Explain.

Optional activity: Direct group members to the activity labeled "Be Angry. Don't Sin?" on page 39. Ask volunteers to share any insights gained or questions considered while completing the activity.

MOVE TO EPHESIANS 4:29-30.

QUESTION 3: How does a church benefit when its members speak with integrity?

This is an observation question that asks the group to discuss the benefits to the church when we are disciplined about the integrity in our words. You might also engage a short discussion associated with how a lack of discipline in words affects church unity.

Optional follow-up: How have you recently benefitted from others who speak with integrity?

QUESTION 4: How does technology amplify the impact of our words?

This question addresses the role social media like Twitter, Facebook, and Instagram and technology like texting play into our connection through words. Many times it's instant, in print, and very public.

Optional follow-up: What are some additional aspects of modern culture that impact the way we communicate with one another?

CONTINUE WITH EPHESIANS 4:31-32.

QUESTION 5: What habits, routines, and choices will empower us to make the changes commanded here?

You will have group members who struggle with these reactions at varying levels. For some it's a life problem and for others it may be more situational. This question is asking both groups for real steps that can be taken to protect our connection through words.

Optional follow-up: "To follow Jesus Christ requires that we relate to others the way He relates to us." Using Ephesians 4:31-32, give specific examples of what this looks like when lived out in day-to-day life.

Note: The following question does not appear in the group member book. Use it in your group discussion as time allows.

QUESTION 6: What obstacles have the potential to hinder us from speaking with integrity each day?

This question requires some transparency. Because of this you'll want to be ready with an example of your own.

LIVE IT OUT

Choosing to speak in a positive way seems easy, but it can be difficult to accomplish. Invite group members to consider these three options for being wise with their words:

- **Speak positively.** Look for opportunities where your words can encourage, motivate, give hope, provide guidance, or even just make someone smile.

- **Memorize Psalm 19:14.** Pray this verse every morning as you prepare for the day ahead. Let it guide your speech.

- **Resolve your dishonesty.** Identify a person with whom you've been dishonest in recent months. Confess your deception, request forgiveness, and affirm your commitment to honest speech moving forward.

Challenge: Words can hurt. But words can also be a powerful force for good. Start each day this next week with a plan for something you will do to bring hope into darkness and connect others with Christ through your words.

Pray: Ask for prayer requests and ask group members to pray for the different requests as intercessors. As the leader, close this time by asking the Lord to help each of you use your words to motivate, encourage, and inspire.

SESSION FIVE: CONNECTED IN SERVICE

The Point: Serving in the church is not about what I want.

The Passage: Ephesians 5:15-21

The Setting: Living out the theology of redemption encompasses much more than observing a brief checklist of "bad" behaviors to replace with "good" ones. It involves a complete lifestyle change—how you walk or live. It means living as wise people rather than continuing to follow the foolish walk of the non-Christian. It means choosing to submit to the Holy Spirit rather than fleshly appetites. It means interacting with other Christians in a manner consistent with your connection to them, that is, the person of Jesus Christ.

QUESTION 1: What's something you always wanted but never got?

Optional activity: Divide participants into two or three subgroups. Instruct each subgroup to design a not-for-profit ministry that could impact the world in a positive way. Use the following questions to help group members think through the different aspects involved in creating such a ministry:

- What would be your ministry's primary purpose?

- How would your ministry be financed?

- What kinds of employees or volunteers would your ministry require?

- What obstacles would you need to overcome in order to get your ministry off the ground?

Call the group back together after 5-10 minutes. As time allows, encourage group members to share the key elements of their ministry ideas.

Video Summary: This week's video message speaks to how we use the time we have to connect through service. The word used in verse 16 for "time" is *kairos*. This word choice is significant because Paul was communicating that we have a finite amount of time and we need to make the most of it. This passage should communicate to us that we need to approach our service as a part of the body with a sense of urgency.

WATCH THE DVD SEGMENT FOR SESSION 5, THEN USE THE FOLLOWING QUESTIONS AND DISCUSSION POINTS TO TRANSITION INTO THE STUDY.

- In what ways does the sense of urgency communicated in this passage change the way you view your responsibility to connect with other believers through service?

- You have a limited amount of time. What will you do with it?

WHAT DOES THE BIBLE SAY?

ASK FOR A VOLUNTEER TO READ ALOUD EPHESIANS 5:15-21.

Response: What's your initial reaction to these verses?

- What questions do you have about these verses?

- What new application do you hope to get from this passage?

TURN THE GROUP'S ATTENTION TO EPHESIANS 5:15-17.

QUESTION 2: Who has been a model of wisdom in your life?

Be sure the group is responding in a way consistent with Ephesians 5:15-17. This question allows group members to unpack their definition of wisdom by describing an individual in their lives.

> ***Optional follow-up:*** How would you define or summarize the concept of wisdom?

MOVE TO EPHESIANS 5:18.

QUESTION 3: What are the implications of being filled by the Spirit on a daily basis?

The emphasis in this question is on the regular, or "daily," practice of being filled by the Spirit. Group members should discuss what this implies about how they should use their time and energy.

> ***Optional follow-up:*** Every Christian is indwelt by the Spirit, but not every Christian heeds the direction and instruction of the Holy Spirit. What are the implications when we don't allow Him to fill us on a daily basis as it relates to serving through the church?

MOVE TO EPHESIANS 5:19-21.

QUESTION 4: What changes must we make in order to serve the way God wants?

Encourage group members to examine the text more closely as they consider changes they can make to become more effective at serving. Point out the differences between an impulse that originates in the heart and a sense of obligation.

> ***Optional follow-up:*** What benefits might you expect personally when you make these changes?

QUESTION 5: What does it mean to submit to one another in the context of a local church?

This question reinforces the point that as church members we must put aside personal stake and gain and submit to one another. You may ask the group to explore the application of "submitting" in their relationships with one another within the body.

> ***Optional follow-up:*** What actions or attitudes empower us to submit in this way?

> ***Optional follow-up:*** What actions or attitudes hinder our ability to demonstrate mutual submission?

Note: The following question does not appear in the group member book. Use it in your group discussion as time allows.

QUESTION 6: What benefits have you received from serving in your local church?

This is an opportunity for group members to share experiences. These experiences are both testimony and teaching moments.

> ***Optional activity:*** Direct group members to the activity labeled "Spending Time" on page 49. Encourage participants to share practical tips for serving others throughout the day.

LIVE IT OUT

Are you a giver or a taker in the body of Christ? Encourage group members to consider these practical ideas for engaging their church the right way:

- **Assess yourself.** Look again at the patterns of self-centered churches listed on pages 48-49. Take a moment to consider whether you contribute to any of these patterns in your church.

- **Accentuate the positive.** Make a list of everything you like best about your local church.

- **Jump in.** Work with leaders at your church to identify a ministry in which your service will meet a need. Then take the plunge and serve with wisdom.

Challenge: Submission is countercultural in the world today. It can be tough to bend our will to God's Spirit— and especially to other members in the body of Christ. But it's worth it. Consciously practice submission this week. Each morning, ask the Lord to guide your thoughts, attitudes, words, and actions. At the end of the week, evaluate how being sensitive to His leading and choosing to submit made a difference in the way you lived.

Pray: Ask for prayer requests and ask group members to pray for the different requests as intercessors. As the leader, close this time by asking the Lord to show each of you how you can more selflessly serve your church.

SESSION SIX: CONNECTED THROUGH PRAYER

The Point: Support your church with prayer.

The Passage: Ephesians 6:18-22

The Setting: As Paul wrapped up his Letter to the Ephesians, he had one last word of instruction before saying his goodbyes: pray. Competing religions and philosophies had not left Ephesus just because Paul wrote to the church there. To successfully stand in their faith and against the evils around them, believers must pray. They must pray at all times. They must pray with perseverance. They must pray for each other. They must pray for those who lead and guide them.

QUESTION 1: What do you miss most when the power goes out?

> **Optional activity:** Begin the group discussion by giving a AAA or AA battery to each participant as a reminder that prayer grants us access to God's power. When each person has a battery, lead the group in an extended time of prayer. Be sure to include a time of praise and thanksgiving directed toward God, as well as a time of intercession where group members share needs and pray for one another.

Video Summary: This last message focuses on how we can connect with others in the body through prayer. Healthy churches are churches made up of members who are praying in the Spirit, at all times. They are directed by God and are always asking Him to help them know how to pray. Prayer reminds us of the needs of others and connects us to others. And as we pray, we are submitting to others and submitting to Him.

WATCH THE DVD SEGMENT FOR SESSION 6, THEN USE THE FOLLOWING QUESTIONS AND DISCUSSION POINTS TO TRANSITION INTO THE STUDY.

- What does it mean to "pray at all times in the Spirit"?
- In what ways does prayer help us stay connected?

WHAT DOES THE BIBLE SAY?

ASK FOR A VOLUNTEER TO READ ALOUD EPHESIANS 6:18-22.

Response: What's your initial reaction to these verses?

- What questions do you have about how you can best support your church through prayer?
- What new application do you hope to get from this passage?

TURN THE GROUP'S ATTENTION TO EPHESIANS 6:18.

QUESTION 2: How does the command to pray at all times influence our daily routines?

This is an interpretation question asked so that group members will better understand the effect of prayer as well as the act of prayer as it relates to their daily lives.

> **Optional follow-up:** What methods or techniques have helped you incorporate prayer into your everyday life?

> **Optional activity:** Direct group members to the activity labeled "Time to Pray" on page 61. Encourage participants to share ideas for more fully incorporating prayer into their routines each day.

MOVE TO EPHESIANS 6:19-20.

QUESTION 3: What keeps us from being more aware of our church leaders' prayer needs?

This question asks the group to consider the ways they can pray for the leaders of their church. Because not all pastors and church staff are openly transparent, church members must be discerning in praying for their leaders.

> **Optional follow-up:** In what areas do you think your leaders need the most prayer support? How do your thoughts compare to the list on page 61?

CONTINUE WITH EPHESIANS 6:21-22.

QUESTION 4: How do we determine and prioritize our prayer needs?

Church members need a process for developing an intercessory prayer life. This includes listening with discernment, asking people how we can pray, and carefully monitoring the people in our lives.

> ***Optional follow-up:*** Where do we draw the line between seeking how to pray for others and sniffing for gossip?

QUESTION 5: How can we use the tools at our disposal to more fully support each other through prayer?

This question is application in nature. You might first begin with a quick list of the available prayer "tools" for communicating prayer needs i.e. email, personal visit, phone call, Internet. Also discuss ways your group can make better use of these tools in remaining connected in prayer.

Note: The following question does not appear in the group member book. Use it in your group discussion as time allows.

QUESTION 6: How do you think transparency and authenticity within your community of believers play into being connected through prayer?

These questions ask group members to consider the role honesty plays in a church's level of connection through prayer. We can't support one another if we don't know what's going on in the lives of each other. You may ask about levels of transparency and challenges to greater levels of authenticity as a part of this question.

> ***Optional follow-up:*** What are you doing to be sure your community of believers knows how to pray for you?

LIVE IT OUT

God works through the prayers of His people. Encourage group members to consider these practical ways to pray for their brothers and sisters in Christ:

- **Pray for salvation.** Many people miss the benefits of church membership because they are not part of the church. Pray for the salvation of at least one person who needs it.

- **Pray for church leaders.** Commit to pray five minutes each day for your pastor(s) and church leaders. (*Note: this works best when you ask them for prayer requests.*)

- **Become educated about at least one missionary's needs.** Pray for that missionary and his or her work every day for at least one month.

Challenge: Prayer grants us access to the power and presence of God. Praying for others is a solemn responsibility and a life-changing promise within the body of Christ. Identify two or three new people you will begin praying for this week. Start by contacting them to ask how you can pray specifically for their needs.

Pray: As the leader, close this final session of *Connected* in prayer. Ask the Lord to help each of you as you move forward to discover or rediscover the joy and privilege that comes from being a committed part of a local church.

WHERE THE BIBLE MEETS LIFE

Bible Studies for Life™ will help you know Christ, live in community, and impact the world around you. If you enjoyed this study, be sure and check out these forthcoming releases.* Six sessions each.

TITLE	RELEASE DATE
Let Hope In *by Pete Wilson*	December 2013
Productive: Finding Joy in What We Do *by Ronnie and Nick Floyd*	December 2013
Connected: My Life in the Church *by Thom S. Rainer*	January 2014
Resilient Faith: Staying Faithful in the Midst of Suffering *by Mary Jo Sharp*	March 2014
Beyond Belief: Exploring the Character of God *by Freddy Cardoza*	March 2014
Overcome: Living Beyond Your Circumstances *by Alex Himaya*	June 2014
Storm Shelter: God's Embrace in the Psalms *by David Landrith*	September 2014
Ready: Ministering Life to Those in Crisis *by Chip Ingram*	September 2014

If your group meets regularly, you might consider Bible Studies for Life as an ongoing series. Available for your entire church—kids, students, and adults—it's a format that will be a more affordable option over time. And you can jump in anytime. For more information, visit **biblestudiesforlife.com**.

biblestudiesforlife.com/smallgroups
800.458.2772 | LifeWay Christian Stores

Title and release dates subject to change.

*This is not a complete list of releases. Additional titles will continue to be released every three months. Visit website for more information.